the *D*ESIRE to

*K*NOW

ALSO BY MICHAELA RILEY KARR

The Allyen

the DESIRE to KNOW

Our Journey to Find My Mother's
Birth Parents

Michaela Riley Karr

Rye Meadow Press

Published by Rye Meadow Press, based in Emporia, KS.
ryemeadowpress@gmail.com

ISBN-13: 978-0-9986065-2-1
Library of Congress Control Number: 2017913133

Cover Design by Magpie Designs, Ltd., © 2017
Photo Credits: Pixabay
Film Strip Image Credit: Ashley Pomeroy
Textures Credit: Sascha Duensing
Author Photo Credit: Jordan Storrer Photography

Printed in the United States of America.
First Edition, 2018.

$\mathcal{D}$EDICATION

For my mother, Cynthia, whom I can never thank
enough. Thanks for letting me go on this journey with
you. I love you.

$\mathcal{C}$ONTENTS

FAMILY TREES

Duvall
(Cynthia's biological mother's side)

Clarence Duvall (1906 – 1971)
    1st Marriage (1928 – 1934) – Sadie Hammonds
    2nd Marriage (1935 – abt. 1939) – Agnes Fahnert
        Carolyn Joy Duvall (b. 1937 in Texas)
    3rd Marriage (1946 – His Death) – Irene Silkoff (see below)
        *Donna Duvall (b. 1947 in Hot Springs, AR)
          Married Ricky Magar.
            *Tracy
            Scott
            *Lisa
        <u>Diana Jean Duvall</u> (b. 1949 in Hot Springs, AR)
          Dated <u>Robert Mark Workman</u> (1963-1965)
            Baby Girl (b. 1965) ←
          Married Duane Robertson
            Brian
            Bridgett

Irene Silkoff (1911 – 1992)
    Unknown Previous Husband
        Erlene Jines (1941 – 2006)
          Married to Bernie Powell
            *Jeff

"*" denotes who we met on our trip to Arkansas in 2017
"_____" denotes Cynthia's biological parents.
"←" denotes Cynthia; Michaela's mother.

i

Workman
(Cynthia's biological father's side)

James and Anna Workman
    Anthony
    Judith
    Trudy
    Steven
    <u>Robert Mark Workman </u>(1946 – 2007)
        Dated <u>Diana Jean Duvall</u> from 1963 to 1965.
            Baby Girl (b. 1965) ←
        Married *Beth Buento in 1966.
            Jay
            *Nicole
    *Kris
    David
    Paul

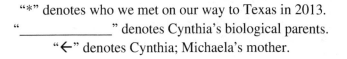

"*" denotes who we met on our way to Texas in 2013.
"_____" denotes Cynthia's biological parents.
"←" denotes Cynthia; Michaela's mother.

*I*NTRODUCTION

*W*ithin these pages is the true story of Cynthia's adoption and our later search for her biological family. It is a journey that both of us have been emotionally invested in for a very long time (thirty-four years for Cynthia, six for Michaela), and only now, in 2017, has God brought our search to an end. Many people have asked us over the years, "How did you find them?", and they have been fascinated by a search that took thousands of hours and hundreds of miles to complete.

We are happy to be able to share with you now all of the details of this special story, far more than either of us could ever tell in person, as well as this priceless journey that we took together.

Please be advised that all names beyond ours have been changed in order to protect the privacy of all individuals involved, as well as the names of the small towns and cities where these events took place. We hope you enjoy learning about the search of a woman who wanted to know who she was and where she came from with the help of her daughter, who, through this search, became closer to her own mother than ever before.

Michaela Riley Karr
Cynthia Giger Riley

PART ONE:
CYNTHIA'S SEARCH

Cynthia

CHAPTER 1:

TURNING EIGHTEEN

I always knew I was adopted. No effort was ever made to hide it, so it was common knowledge that both my brother and I were adopted. There were a lot of children's books about adoption in our house for my brother and I to read whenever we had questions.

Adoption was rather common in my extended family as well, but I loved my family to pieces and still do to this day. My parents were not perfect, but they tried. However, as I grew older, so did my desire to know. To know what my story was. To know why I was given up. To know who I was.

In the 1960s, all adoptions were closed. Little to no information was shared between the biological and adoptive parents. It was so different than it is nowadays. I knew the adoption agency, but that was it. It was very hard to wait until I was eighteen to discover more. All I knew was that I was born in December of 1965 in Wichita, Kansas, and, less than a month later, I was adopted to my parents and renamed Cynthia Giger. Until then, I had an itch to know, and it could not be scratched by anything else.

I turned eighteen in 1983, and the very first thing I did was send a letter to the adoption agency for my original birth certificate. Of course, I had one with my adoptive parents' names on it, but, to me, my first step was to get the original and see if it had a name or two on it. Maybe, it would tell me something about who I was. Maybe, I could find my birth parents, even though I knew in the back of my mind that it would be impossible because of how closed adoptions were back then.

When the certificate came in the mail, I couldn't believe my eyes. It had my birth mother's name on it. Her signature that she signed with her own hand. I could read words that my own birth mother wrote, and I cried at the sight, tracing my finger along the letters.

Diana Jean Duvall.

To me, it was the very first step of knowing her. A signature was so personal, but my birth certificate held a plethora of other information that I had never known. She was sixteen years old at the time of my birth. Only fifteen when I was likely conceived. She was born in Hot Springs, Arkansas. Not only that, but it had addresses. One was her home address, where she had lived in 1965. An avenue named after a fruit in Parsons, Kansas. Not terribly far from Wichita where I had lived my whole life. Her street sounded like such a nice place to grow up, so I couldn't help but hope that maybe I was born to a nice girl who just made a mistake. The other address on the birth certificate was her current mailing address, one in Wichita. When I researched it, it came back as a home for unwed mothers.

My heart sank as I read the space for the father's name and saw the words typewritten, "Name withheld by mother." She did not give his name. This sent my mind whirling with questions and concerns. Did she know who he was? Or, was she trying to protect him?

Still yet, was this simply what was done in the '60s?

Shame began to trickle through my system. What if she wasn't a nice girl? What if I was the product of the sin of pre-marital sex? Or worse. Hundreds of possibilities flew through my head. Date rape. Incest. Sexual abuse. My desire to know the answers compounded in only seconds. I knew as a Christian woman that I was an adopted daughter of the one true King, but for reasons not entirely clear to me, my mind craved to know if I was at least a product of love.

As I absorbed everything on the birth certificate, I also began to feel excited and at a loss at the same time. I knew her name and her 1965 address. Where did I go from here? There was no name for my father. Would I ever discover who he was? I had learned so much and yet so little. Not knowing how to even go about searching, I decided my best option was to leave a letter at the agency. That way, if Diana ever searched for me, they could give it to her. I prayed that she would find me since I didn't know where to even begin.

My search flatlined as I became busy with college. It didn't pick up again until the summer of 1986, slightly unintentionally. That was the year I decided to transfer from Mid-America Nazarene University in Olathe to Kansas Newman back in Wichita so that I would be closer to home. I wanted to be a nurse, and Kansas Newman wouldn't allow me into nursing school without a health history.

To be quite honest, it blew my mind. In the past, whenever someone had asked me for a health history, all I had to say was "I'm adopted" and everything was fine. I didn't know what my health history was, much less who I was. Of course, I wasn't about to let go of my dreams of being a nurse, and so I paid the fifty dollars to my old adoption agency to send me the information.

That fifty dollars got me so much more than I ever imagined. Far more information than I even knew existed. Those pages upon pages of health statistics gave me such a better picture of who my birth family was. I learned that my birth mother was born in August of 1949, that she was Methodist, and of German and French descent. She worked as a concessions girl, and played the piano. She was 5'4" with blonde hair and brown eyes, just like me. From

Michaela Riley Karr

The health history information sheet for Cynthia's birth mother, Diana Jean Duvall.

KANSAS CHILDREN'S SERVICE LEAGUE

INFORMATION ABOUT BABY'S MOTHER

(Write in ink or type)

DATE *Nov. 18, 1965*

NAME

ADDRESS

BIRTH DATE *Aug.* ▓ *1949* BIRTH PLACE ▓ *Arkansas*

NATIONALITY *German + French* RELIGION *Methodist*

EDUCATION *11th grade* OCCUPATIONAL HISTORY *Concession girl*

TALENTS AND INTERESTS *music — some piano*

HEIGHT *5'4"* WEIGHT ▓ *93* COLOR EYES *brown* COLOR HAIR *blonde* CURLY *yes*

COMPLEXION *light* FACE SHAPE *oval* WEAR GLASSES *no* DENTAL PROBLEMS *yes - partial plate*

ILLNESSES: TB *no* CONVULSIONS *no* HAY FEVER *no* BLEEDING TENDENCIES *no*

ASTHMA *no* RHEUMATIC FEVER *no* JAUNDICE PROBLEMS *no*

CHILDHOOD DISEASES *yes - measles* OPERATIONS *knee operation osteomyelitis - no recur*

FAMILY ILLNESSES: TB *no* DIABETES *no* EPILEPSY *no*

ALLERGIES *yes* HEART *yes* CANCER *yes* RHEUMATIC FEVER *no*

MENTAL ILLNESS *no* MENTAL RETARDATION *no*

BIRTH DEFECTS *none* OTHER

MARRIED *no* DIVORCED *no* SINGLE *yes*

Date and place

HUSBAND'S NAME

DOES HE KNOW OF PREGNANCY *yes* HIS ATTITUDE

FIRST PREGNANCY *yes* HOW MANY ___ NO. OF CHILDREN LIVING

there, it was simple medical questions that she answered yes or no to, but at the bottom of the page, she wrote that the birth father knew about her pregnancy. The space for "His Attitude" was left blank.

On the next page, I learned about her immediate family. Aside from the fact that she had a grandfather who died of a heart attack and a grandmother who died of cancer, I discovered for the first time that Diana had two older sisters. One of whom would have been in high school with her. Her father ran the local movie theater. She must have worked concessions at his theater.

To my surprise, the next pages held the same kind of information for my birth father! He was three years older than Diana; a 6'2", blond-haired, blue-eyed Catholic boy of German descent who was at college studying to be a mechanic. He had been born in Parsons, and had four brothers and three sisters of varying ages. He had admitted paternity, but had given no financial support. He had claimed responsibility, I thought. Not many men did that back then.

To my intense disappointment, every name that

Michaela Riley Karr

The health history information sheet for Cynthia's birth father.

DATE *Nov 18, 1965*

BABY'S FATHER _____

ADDRESS _____

BIRTH DATE *Sept* ___ BIRTH PLACE ███████ *Kansas* NATIONALITY *German*

EDUCATION *High School*

OCCUPATION *Student in college (Freshman)*

TALENTS AND INTERESTS *cars + mechanics*

RELIGION *Catholic* MARITAL STATUS *single*

DOES HE KNOW OF PREGNANCY *yes* ADMITTED PATERNITY *yes* DENIED _____

GIVEN FINANCIAL ASSISTANCE *no*

HEIGHT *6'3"* WEIGHT *185* COLOR EYES *blue* COLOR HAIR *blonde* CURLY *yes*

FACE SHAPE *round* COMPLEXION *dark* WEAR GLASSES *yes* DENTAL PROBLEMS _____

FATHER'S ILLNESSES: TB *no* DIABETES ███ *no* CONVULSIONS *no*

GIVEN FINANCIAL ASSISTANCE *no*

HEIGHT *6'3"* WEIGHT *185* COLOR EYES *blue* COLOR HAIR *blonde* CURLY *yes*

FACE SHAPE *round* COMPLEXION *dark* WEAR GLASSES *yes* DENTAL PROBLEMS _____

FATHER'S ILLNESSES: TB *no* DIABETES ███ *no* CONVULSIONS *no*

FAMILY ILLNESSES: TB *no* DIABETES *yes* CONVULSIONS *no*

BLEEDING TENDENCIES _____ RHEUMATIC FEVER _____ JAUNDICE PROBLEMS _____

HAY FEVER _____ ASTHMA _____ MENTAL ILLNESS _____ MENTAL RETARDATION _____

BIRTH DEFECTS _____ OTHER _____

had ever been on the documents had been whited out. Even my birth mother's name, which I already knew from my original birth certificate. I would continually stare at where my birth father's name had once been, trying to guess the swirls of the letters that I could still see above and below the white-out.

Most surprising of all was the final page of the packet of papers they sent me. It was the "Reason for Adoptive Placement" page. It talked about how my birth mother had two older sisters, the eldest of whom was living in a different state, and that her parents were very supportive during her pregnancy. The family had only lived in Parsons for two years, and the middle sister had come to the unwed mothers' home to be with Diana. So she wouldn't be scared, I figured. I always thought that was really sweet, before I eventually knew the truth.

Down below, it said that they decided to put me up for adoption because both my birth parents were in school. They felt it would be best for everyone involved. The agency made sure to add on the fact that it was extremely unacceptable for a single woman to raise a baby in the '60s.

Also included in the packet of papers was the court

order where I was surrendered. Her signature that gave me away. I could understand her giving me away. I really could. I couldn't imagine being a sixteen-year-old mother. Yet, once again, even though I was provided with so much more information, I had so many more questions. The fierce desire to know and to find them was not quenched.

It so happened that the fifty dollars I paid for my health history also included an offer by the adoption agency to do a search for Diana. As time went by, I was very hopeful that they would find her. That she would still be in Parsons or somewhere else close to Wichita. That by some impossible way, they would find my birth father too.

Nothing could have prepared me for the information they brought back. They sent me a letter telling how Diana and her entire family had moved to California to be with her eldest sister who lived there. California was so far from Wichita. Totally inaccessible for me.

To me, that news meant the end of my search. It wasn't like I could drive to California. Facebook did not exist, and the world wide web was only just getting started. I could not simply search online to secretly find a picture or something. The fifty dollars did allow me to call the agency back at any time in order to keep my information up to date, but other than that, I felt certain that there would be no feasible way for me to find her.

That was 1986. It was 1990 before I called the agency again. I had gotten married and decided to update my name and address in case by some happenstance Diana wanted to find me. Other than that, my search went cold for a long time. I didn't want to give up, but I had no idea what to do.

All I knew for sure was my desire to know. My desire to know what these people were like even if I never got to meet them. My desire to see pictures of people who looked like me, something I never experienced in my whole life until my children were born. I wanted to know Diana and my birth father's full story, not just what the adoption agency had given me.

People never really understood my desire to know. They would ask me, "Why are you doing this?" and "What do you expect to get out of this?" These questions hurt whenever I heard them, but I didn't care. No one could squash my desire to know, and I would respond with a smile and say, "Because it makes me happy." It was as simple as that. Even if I never got anywhere, the search still made me happy to be trying.

Little did I know that an opportunity to travel to where it all began was knocking at my door.

$\mathcal{C}$HAPTER 2:

THE FIRST TRIP

$\mathcal{I}$n 1992, God opened a door for me to continue my search. I had been married for two years, and we were living in Overland Park, Kansas, near Kansas City. My husband was an accountant, and he happened to have a client down in southeastern Kansas. I was charged with the task of taking some accounting records to this client, and at this point in my life, I was so very ready to take the next step. I didn't want to have to wait for Diana to find me. Therefore, I decided to day trip to Parsons on my way home.

It was summertime. It was very hot, and my mind

was filled with anxious thoughts as I drove down the highway. I was dressed in my Sunday best, and I had applied my makeup with care, just in case. Nonetheless, that didn't stop me from worrying, so I tried to think through my plan. It was simple enough. I was going to go to Parsons High School and ask if they had any old yearbooks. Then I could maybe get the pictures that I had craved for so long.

As I pulled into the parking lot, my heart was about to hammer out of my chest. I was terrified and feeling very vulnerable. I was in a city I'd never been to before, heading to a building that I'd never stepped foot inside to do something that was very personal. School was out for the summer. I didn't even know if the door would be unlocked. I began to wonder if I should just head home and not even try.

However, my desire to know was simply not going to allow me to do that. I mustered every ounce of courage that I could and got out of my truck. I tottered over to the front door and pulled. It was open. I tried not to look like a deer caught in headlights as I entered the building. The building where both of my birth parents had spent their high school years. I was somewhere they had been, and I couldn't shake the thrill that overcame me. It was the first time that I had ever stepped foot into a building that my birth mother had also been in, as well as the first step toward feeling like I, whoever I was, existed. It was exciting and comforting to walk where she once walked.

At least until I entered the front office. There sat a secretary, an older woman who was likely trying to get some things done before she could head home for the day. I nervously approached her counter and asked if they had any old yearbooks, '63, '64, and '65 in particular.

The secretary seemed more than willing to help, and she disappeared into the back. As the minutes ticked on, my thoughts sped up. Soon, it felt like she had been gone an hour. I second guessed myself every second. What was I doing here? Why had I come here? I wondered what thoughts were going through the secretary's mind.

Did she think I was crazy? Worse yet, did she think that I was a bad person for trying to dig up somebody else's dirty laundry? I felt like a stalker. Could somebody arrest me for that? Every anxious thought possible soared through my mind.

So much time went by that I actually considered

leaving before the secretary came back with the three exact editions of the yearbook that I needed. Rather than becoming relieved, my anxiety only heightened. The secretary led me to the library, which was completely empty, where I could sit at a table and chair.

Surrounded by dark, dusty bookshelves and armed with a notepad and a film camera, I cracked the first one open. I knew exactly what I was looking for: Diana Duvall, a sister either two or three years older, and every senior boy that had a younger sister about the same age as Diana. I knew my birth father had a sister that age from the health history form.

After checking both the '63 and '64 yearbooks with no luck, I couldn't believe it when I found her picture. Diana was a sophomore in the 1965 yearbook. It was a black and white picture. Her hair was cut into the classic beehive hairstyle, which I could somewhat tell was blonde like the health history information had said. Her eyes looked like mine, and her face shape was similar. There was a slight smile on her face, as if she hadn't quite been ready when the camera snapped the photo, not unlike most school pictures. I think I took five or six pictures of her photo with my camera.

Unlike with today's technology, I would have to have the photos developed later, and I wanted to be absolutely certain that I had gotten a picture of her, my mother.

In the same yearbook, I found Diana's older sister. Her name was Donna, and she was a senior in 1965. She looked different from Diana because she had dark hair and a different face shape. Donna was actually in all three of the yearbooks I asked for since she was older.

I also flipped to a picture of the choir at PHS since the health history indicated that Diana was interested in music. Lo and behold, she was in the front row. She wasn't smiling, but most of the people in the picture weren't. If I hadn't known any better, I would have said that I was looking at a picture of myself in my high school choir. It tingled my senses to be looking at someone who looked so much like me. I had never experienced that in my entire life.

Along with the multiple pictures I took of Diana and her sister, Donna, I took pictures and notes over six to eight boys who were the correct age and had a younger sister the correct age. I couldn't help but finger my notepad and think to myself that one of these young men had to be my birth father.

After gleaning every bit of information I possibly could from those three yearbooks, I returned them to the secretary and headed back to my truck with a camera full of priceless pictures and a notepad etched with names to search for.

Just to make sure I hit all my bases, I drove to the public library to search their microfiche, or their negatives of old newspapers. I looked up my birth father's date of birth, which I knew from the health history forms, in order to search for some sort of birth announcement. Maybe, it would help narrow down my list of six to eight boys, I thought. No such luck. I even searched the entire week of his birth, but there weren't any birth announcements. Nothing. I tried not to let this bother me, since I had a whole list to work from that I felt so sure contained the right name.

Therefore, I left the library and went to the local Quik-Trip to use their payphone to get started. They always had massive phonebooks chained to them, and so I parked my truck as close as physically possible to that payphone so I could thumb through the phonebook.

Of all the men on my little list, only one of them

still lived in Parsons. Hope surged through me. What were the odds of his being the only one still in Parsons? I couldn't help but think that God was guiding me to my birth father. I found my way to that address in the phonebook, feeling more and more anxious than I ever had in the high school office. This was a whole new level of being a stalker in my mind.

Nobody was home when I arrived, so I parked my truck across the street and waited. Every moment I anxiously wondered if I should leave, and I began to feel paranoid. After fifteen or twenty minutes passed, I decided that even if he was home, I wasn't brave enough to go up to his front door. So, I wrote a letter in my notepad. It was very basic, just explaining who I was and that I was looking for Diana Jean Duvall and my birth father. I gave him all the details I had at that point, which wasn't much. I don't remember exactly, but I don't believe I asked specifically if he was my birth father in my letter. I was too afraid. I left my address and my phone number in the letter, just in case he reached out to me.

By the time I finished writing it, a car had pulled into his driveway. A whole little family got out, looking as if they had just spent a fun day at the pool.

There were a lot of little girls in swimsuits tugging along floaties. An older gentleman climbed out of the passenger seat of the car, holding one of these little girls' hands as they walked toward his house, and I knew it had to be him.

Quickly swallowing my fear, I got out of my truck and strode across the street like a woman on a mission. He looked confused, but I walked right up to him and handed him my letter. All I could muster was, "My name is Cynthia Riley, and I would really appreciate it if you could read this. Thank you for your time." That was it. I didn't have the guts to say anything else. I had most definitely used up my bravery for the day. I turned around, got back in my truck, and drove back to Kansas City.

I don't remember whether he called or wrote, but a few months later, he contacted me. He had no idea who Diana Jean Duvall even was. I was absolutely crushed. I thought finding him in the phonebook was my sign from God that he was the right one. Or, that he could at least help me find Diana. He even showed up during the thirty minutes that I sat outside his house. What were the odds of that?

I was thoroughly frustrated with myself that I was

not brave enough to ask him, "Are you my father?" I wanted it to be like a Hallmark movie where everything worked out perfectly and everyone had a happy ending. Where was my happy ending?

I begged God a lot to help me during that time; however, this experience soon became only the first. As the years went by, no one I ever asked knew who the Duvalls were, much less who Diana was. It was always the same answer: "Never heard of her" and "Didn't know her." All of my early search days ended like this. It started to make me feel as if Diana never existed. And if Diana never existed, then neither did I.

In 1994 and 1997, my children, Michaela and Matthew, were born. When Michaela was born, she was the spitting image of her father. Olive skin and dark hair. Someone actually walked up to me in Wal-Mart while I had her with me and asked me why I'd married a foreigner. When she was a baby, the only way she resembled me was that she had my eyes, and I clung to that fiercely. Yet, when we wanted to get pregnant again, I threatened my husband to think recessive because I wanted a baby who looked more like me. I'd never had someone who looked like me.

Luckily for him, it worked. Matthew was pale-skinned with blond hair and brown eyes, just like me. I could look at him and see myself, and likewise see Diana. Of course, as they've grown, they've become a mix of my husband and I rather than one or the other, but I was very desperate to have someone that looked like me. I've often said that the greatest gift my children ever gave me was the fact that I can see myself in them.

My search mostly fell apart after my trip to Parsons in 1992. In 1999, I was a nursing professor, and I happened to have a student who was from Parsons. We were talking one day and I slowly told her about how I was searching for my birth parents and about the trip I had taken to Parsons years prior. My student was very interested in my search, but upon hearing that I went to the high school, she asked, "Did you know there is a Catholic high school in Parsons, too?"

It was almost like a slap in the face. Why did I not check for more than one high school when I was there in '92? My health history paperwork said that my birth father was Catholic. I knew right then and there that all the high school boys on my notepad at home had to be wrong. I felt so stupid. All I wanted in life was to go back to Parsons to see if the Catholic high school had any yearbooks I could look at, but I knew that there was no way. In 1999, we had two small children and didn't have any extra money lying around. There was no way to even get back to Parsons now.

My mind whirled with all the possibilities, but by the time I got home that evening, I knew I had to let go of my search. As far as I knew, Diana was nearly two thousand miles away in California. I had no way of acquiring an address or a phone number. California was a massive state and every search for Diana Duvall I did came up empty-handed. I couldn't even search for my birth father without a name. There was nothing more I could do now, except pray that one of them would try to find me. These facts gave me a deep sadness that lasted a very long time.

Michaela was just entering kindergarten as I buried my search and my desire to know. In 1999, the world wide web was only just getting to the point of being considered a source. I could never have known that in twelve years, my then five-year-old would become the biggest proponent in reviving my search with the help of a much bigger internet.

PART TWO:

OUR JOURNEY TOGETHER

Michaela

CHAPTER 3:

LEARNING THE ROPES

When I was little, I remember being shocked that my mom was adopted. I had just never considered it before, and in my young mind, I always thought she looked like her parents, my grandparents.

She took me up to her bedroom once to show me her manila envelope full of the pictures she took of the Parsons yearbook, of her birth mother and her birth mother's older sister, Diana and Donna. I don't remember how old I was when this happened, maybe thirteen or fourteen, but I do remember thinking that I felt sorry for her. I wished I knew how to help her.

She always used to tell me that the greatest gift my

brother and I ever gave her was the fact that we look like her. To be honest, I couldn't understand it. I grew up my entire life among my dad's extended family. I was able to see myself easily in both my parents, in both my brothers (I have an older brother from Dad's side), and in my grandparents on the Riley side. The Riley side as a whole is ninety-percent olive-skinned, dark-haired, and brown-eyed. I had a ton of people that looked like me, and as I got older, it made me feel guilty that I had too many to count while Mom only had two.

During the summer of 2011, between my junior and senior years of high school, we had our annual family reunion in central Kansas. I was seventeen then, and I had always entertained a pretty big interest in our family history and where we came from. My grandma organized this family reunion every year during the last weekend of July, and she still does to this day. In my opinion, it is also typically the hottest weekend of the whole summer.

When I was little, we would try to go play on the playground next door. We'd burn our hands, feet, and rears on all the old, blistering metal equipment until we gave up and went back inside. Of course, a few years ago, the city installed a splash pad right next to it. I envy my little cousins now, but that's not important.

My wonderful grandmother had boxes upon boxes of family histories and documents that she would lug all the way to reunion every year. I remember always helping my dad and brother carry them in from the car. By age seventeen, playing on the ridiculously hot playground was beyond me, and so that was the first year I actually spent my time looking at those dozens of documents within my grandma's boxes. My brother and I were usually the only ones of our generation to attend, so we often didn't have many people to talk to.

Thus, I spent the full three hours of that reunion day looking at family histories I had never seen before. However, love my grandma as I do, all of these various booklets and documents were in no real order. Or, I should say, in no order I could recognize. Anyone who knows me well can see where this is going. That day, I promised myself that I would not only get Grandma's documents into order, but that I would also digitize them. I wanted to be my family's next kinkeeper, just like my grandma is now.

When we returned home from reunion, I signed up

for my very first Ancestry.com membership. I spent the two or three weeks before my senior year of high school tirelessly digitizing my grandmother's numerous boxes of family records and linking them up to the information I found on Ancestry. It was a lot of fun, really. As soon as I got back far enough, other people had done a lot of my work for me. All I had to do was check to make sure it aligned with Grandma's documents, and then copy and paste.

For the Riley side, I got back to the year 1495 with a man called Thomas Ryley de Sourbi, who lived in Yorkshire, England. He is my 14th great grandfather. As for the Rodgers, my grandma's side, I could only get back to three brothers in Delaware who served in the Revolution because the British burned all our records in the war. That was where Grandma got stuck, too. Darn you, British!

This whole process turned me into a massive history buff. Not even joking. I actually considered getting a double major in history, but that's beside the point.

Ancestry memberships come in six-month and one-year installments. I can't remember which one of these I chose the first time around, but it only took me a month to digitize all of my grandma's things. She was thrilled to see everything I had discovered that branched off of the work she had done, and it was a wonderful, bonding experience for my grandma and I. However, I still had months left of a membership that I had paid a decent sum for. I didn't want it to go to waste.

To this day, I don't remember if it was my idea or Mom's idea, but I do remember us making the decision that we would try. She brought me her precious manila envelope from the firebox upstairs and placed it in my custody while I did my search. I remember feeling very grown up. I was still seventeen and was only a couple of months into my senior year of high school at this point.

I didn't have a ton of information to work with. Just the health history forms that Mom received when she paid for them. It drove me nuts to stare at the whited-out names. By now, I had become very proficient at finding the things I needed on Ancestry, but I had never conducted a search before without names. Those were imperative to finding anything. I began to feel like this search was beyond my capabilities as a seventeen-year-old girl.

Months went by. I focused on Diana, as well as the sister we had a name for, Donna. They were really the only two I knew how to search for at that point. I learned rapidly that it was far more difficult to find people in the twentieth century than in the centuries preceding it.

There is a law that says that each U.S. Census can only be released seventy-two years after it was conducted in order to protect the individuals within. In 2011, the most recent census I had available to me was 1930. If I waited long enough, the 1940 Census was slated to come out the next year in 2012, but that didn't help me much. Diana was born in 1949, Donna around 1946 or 1947, and I had no idea what their parents' names were. They were whited-out too.

Refusing to give up, I began to expand my search beyond Ancestry. Google became my best friend. It gave me at least four or five specific people search websites, but no matter how many times I typed in "Diana J. Duvall", there were always zero results. There were always hundreds of other Dianas who lived in the United States with different last names and ages, but that didn't help me. I didn't even know what state to put in to help narrow it down because while Mom had been told they were in California, I was hesitant to believe this without concrete evidence. I even tried Whitepages.com. Nothing. No Duvalls.

I immediately began to understand what Mom had been dealing with since 1983. At every turn, the answer given was zilch. Nothing. Sorry, the person you're looking for doesn't exist. However, as the months went on, I slowly came to the realization that firstly, Diana had to be alive. Otherwise I would have found a death record or an obituary. And secondly, she had to have married. Therefore, what Mom and I had found out was true: Diana Duvall didn't exist anymore. But Diana So-and-So had to exist. We just had to find her.

Probably in October of 2011, I made a small breakthrough on a website called Findagrave.com. The website is the largest catalog of all cemeteries in the United States, and so I typed in the last name of Duvall into the search as well as the birth year of 1906. In Mom's health history, it listed the full birthdates of each of Diana's parents. By now, I had decided I needed to find a male Duvall. Someone whose name would never change, and judging by the birth year, her father would definitely be dead by now.

One hundred and sixty-seven results popped up. It was extremely overwhelming, but I was bound and determined to help my mother find her heritage and satisfy her desire to know. Thankfully for me, I found who I was looking for on the first page. Clarence H. Duvall had died in 1971, and his wife, Irene, had died in 1992. Both spouses' birthdates matched the ones on the health history form, so I was one-hundred percent sure they were the correct people. They were buried in Batesville, Arkansas.

This discovery was huge. Mom was ecstatic when I told her, because this was the first real proof either of us had ever found that showed that the Duvall family even existed. I'm not sure I can even effectively convey how much this finding of two people's gravestone rejuvenated us and encouraged us to continue searching. Diana's parents were real, and so she had to be real, too.

Over the next couple of months, I busied myself trying to research Clarence and Irene as much as I possibly could. To my delight, I found that Clarence had spent pretty much his whole life in Hot Springs, Arkansas, which I knew was Diana's birthplace from

Mom's paperwork. It reaffirmed to me that he was truly her father. The only thing that gave me lapse was the fact that in the 1930 Census, the most recent one I had access to until around May of 2012, he was married to a woman named Sadie. Not Irene.

However, it wasn't long before I found marriage and divorce records for not only this Sadie, but also his second wife, Agnes. I remember spending hours searching for Agnes because I never found a divorce record for her. Alas, I never found her and assumed that she had died.

Irene was actually Clarence's third wife, whom he didn't marry until after he returned from World War II. On Findagrave.com, it had pictures of their headstone and Clarence's footstone for serving in the army, so I was able to find his military records on Ancestry. Every record I found continued to corroborate Mom's health history forms, so we were encouraged. I tried to keep Mom in the loop as much as I could, but I think it was mind-boggling to her how many records and websites I was juggling between. I started only telling her things once I found information worthy of telling her.

It was nearing November at this point. I had

searched Clarence and Irene as thoroughly as anybody could. I'd found their gravesite, his previous marriages, and his military records. I had found them on every census from 1910 to 1930. Yet, no Diana. And no Donna, and no second older sister that the health history form mentioned either.

Having no idea what to do next, I took Mom's notepad of the six to eight high school seniors that she thought could possibly be her birth father. She explained to me that there was a Catholic high school in Parsons that she'd never known about, but those names were all I had, so I researched them anyway.

Every single one of them came back wrong somehow. Wrong birthdate, wrong number of siblings, wrong marriage date, or wrong appearance. I reached yet another dead end, and I felt like pulling my hair out. I was juggling school, my cashier job at Hy-Vee, marching band, and this search. I desperately wanted it to work, but I found myself wondering if I was doomed just like my mom had been. I felt like Ancestry had failed me after it had yielded so much information during my digitizing of my grandma's records and now gave nothing that would help.

Until I came up with a new plan of action, I wasn't

about to let my Ancestry membership go to waste. So, I began searching the genealogies of Clarence and Irene, so I could give my mom at least part of her heritage. I didn't get far with the Duvalls, just to a guy named Caesar born in 1758 France.

I searched Irene's side, but I didn't know until 2017 that I never had the right maiden name. It turned out that I had her married name from her second marriage. She was married three times too, but I didn't figure that out until later down the road.

I learned rather quickly that as soon as a woman got married, her maiden name dropped off the face of the planet. That's why I had the wrong name for Irene, and why I couldn't find either Diana or Donna. I think this is why I have continued to use my maiden name in my pen name as an author and on my college diplomas. I adore my husband and his family, but I don't want people to forget that I was a Riley before I was a Karr. If one of my descendants ever takes up family history like I did, I want them to be able to find me.

During Christmas break, about four months into my search, I had reached the end of my rope. I didn't know what else to try. I was at a dead end, and even though Mom kept trying to give me ideas of what to try next, I had either already tried them all or there was no physical way to try them. I felt guilty. I felt like a failure that I had been unable to do this for my mother after everything that she had done for me. I was ready to quit.

The last time I opened Mom's laptop to log on to Ancestry, I had a random thought. I had tried finding Diana, but I was at a dead end for now. I hadn't tried searching for her birth father beyond the names I was given yet. Of course, I had no names to try anymore. I didn't even have the birthdates for his parents, which was how I found Diana's parents. The one bit of information that could possibly help me was the birth father's birthdate.

So, in my desperation and feelings of hopelessness, I logged onto Ancestry, cleared all the search criteria, and simply typed in his birthday and Parsons, Kansas. No name, no family members, or any of the other blank fields Ancestry has to offer. Just six digits and a town. To be honest, I was one hundred percent sure that it wouldn't work.

I guess God has a sense of humor.

CHAPTER 4:

FINDING MARK

*T*he one and only hit was an obituary. It was a name I had never seen before. Robert Mark Workman. I glanced at the health history forms, which never left my side during those months, and peered at the whited-out name on his page. Looking at the upper swirls and lower swirls that were left behind, I was skeptical that this name fit. But, it was the first result, it was the right birthday, and it said Parsons, Kansas, so I couldn't not read it. Today, I am very thankful that I did.

Mark (we found out later that he went by his middle name) had been born on the correct date in

1946 in Parsons, Kansas, had worked for the railroad, and was Catholic. As I read further and further, I became more and more convinced that this could be the right guy, but I was sold when I reached the bottom.

He had four brothers and three sisters, all with the exact, corresponding ages as to the health history form in my hands. I think I nearly dropped the laptop. What were the odds of having this much information match? I remember thanking God that his family had published such a thorough obituary. Some obituaries could be rather vague, but this one was at least three paragraphs long.

I remember I started screaming for my mom. Of course, she came running thinking I was dying or something. It wasn't until she reached the room that I realized I had to tell her that it was an obituary. That he had died four years prior in 2007 of leukemia. That there would be no way for her to ever meet him. I think all I could say was, "I've found an obituary, and I'm almost positive he's your birth father."

I could tell that Mom was shocked. I don't think she ever considered that either of her birth parents could be dead. After all, he died at 61, which is rather young. But she couldn't deny all the matching information in the obituary either. There was really no chance that this guy couldn't be him, but we were still a little hesitant. Remembering my success using Findagrave.com, I decided to search for his grave. He was buried in Parsons, but more importantly, his record had a picture of him before he passed. To this day, I have never seen another Findagrave.com entry with a photo of the person, so I know God was helping us.

He looked like my mom. It was in the shape of his face, his eyes, and his lips. He had blue eyes and a little bit of white hair around his bald spot. It was just a headshot, really, we couldn't see much else. Mom couldn't see the resemblance as much, but I could.

It took a little while for Mom to absorb the fact that we had found her birth father. She never dreamed that we would ever find him, much less find him before Diana. It was devastating that he was gone, and it took her a while to work through that. In the end, we would have never found him without the obituary. Sometimes, I still can't believe how it all unfolded. How the obituary was so detailed, and how perfectly it aligned with the paperwork we had to assure us that it was the right man. We give God all the glory.

The obituary also gave us the names of his wife and his two grown children with her. Her name was Beth, and they had gotten married in 1966, almost exactly one year after my mom was born. It took less than five minutes to find them on Facebook. They had pretty high security settings, but we could at least see their profile pictures.

We had reached a crossroads. We found Mark, whom we were ninety-nine percent sure was her birth father. But what did we do from here? It was one thing to spend hours on a laptop researching random people and looking for matching information. It was another thing entirely to start contacting these people and asking if they'd had a baby out of wedlock back in the '60s.

Mom was terrified. What if Beth didn't know? If Mark truly was her birth father, what if he had never told his wife? Or his children? This was family ruination material, and Mom and I were certainly not out to go ruin a family forever. We were torn between our desperation to know and our terror that they would hate us forever for tearing apart their family.

Mom decided that she was going to have to think and pray about what her next step would be.

The rest of Christmas break went by, and I returned to school. I searched for Diana on and off as the months went on, but nothing ever turned up. During that time, Mom decided that she would write letters to the two siblings closest in age to Mark, his older brother, Steve, and his younger sister, Kris. We found their addresses on Whitepages. We figured that his siblings were more likely to know if Mark had fathered a child in 1965, and so, for the time being, we contented ourselves with hoping there would be responses to the letters.

Sometime during the spring of 2012, Mom decided to take the next step and asked to be friends with Beth, Mark's widow, on Facebook. She figured that it wouldn't hurt, and then maybe she could see more pictures. She also sent her a separate message that was rather vague, trying to be as careful as possible and testing the waters to see if Beth knew anything without ruining her life if she didn't. It was a very stressful time trying to craft that message, and it went unanswered for a very long time.

In July of 2012, we decided to rekindle our search

for Diana. I was out of school for the summer, and I had more time to devote to the search. We had found Mark when it seemed like he was the most impossible of the two, so Mom was bound and determined to find Diana.

We created a Facebook page filled with the information that we knew and the pictures that we had. It had her birthdate, her birthplace of Hot Springs, Arkansas, that she had spent high school in Parsons, Kansas, and that her last known destination was California. Social media had really picked up speed in those years, and so we were confident that somehow we could get the page on someone's radar. Someone who knew where Diana was, or even just knew that she existed.

In the meantime, the summer went by. I started school at Emporia State University in the fall of 2012 and met my future husband within three weeks. My Ancestry membership had long since expired, and my focus was solidly on my schoolwork. It was the middle of the semester when I heard from Mom that Beth had finally accepted her friend request, a full nine months after sending it. I was so surprised for her, and yet, my anxiety heightened.

This was it. This was our first contact with someone we were pretty confident was related to Mom's birth family. I couldn't help but feel like we were walking on eggshells, and I worried about what my mom would say while I was an hour and a half away and couldn't help her craft messages. Mom and Beth began talking slowly, but their conversations soon flowed like a massive waterfall. Nothing could have prepared us for all of the revelations Beth had in store for us.

Beth knew. She had known even before my mom was born, because she and Mark started dating while Diana was still in the unwed mothers' home in Wichita. She told us how every Friday, as soon as Mark got his paycheck, he would drive over to Diana's parents' house and give Clarence, her father, his payment toward funding Diana's stay in the unwed mothers' home. Mark had contributed at least half of Diana's funds, but Clarence never told Diana, which is why she marked on her forms that she'd received no financial support from the father of her child. This was a huge surprise for us.

Beth told us how Clarence was not a very nice man, and that he forbade Diana and Mark from speaking to each other ever again. While Diana thought that Mark didn't care and didn't want to help, it was actually her father making those decisions and hiding the truth from her. It was heartbreaking. She was sequestered miles away from her family and her boyfriend. Sixteen, pregnant, and alone, although we still thought at this point in time that her sister, Donna, was there to keep her company.

When Mom was born, a picture of her was sent to Mark, and he kept it in the family album with the rest of their family's pictures. Mark and Beth's children grew up seeing the baby in their photo album, but never knew who she was. When they were around sixteen, Mark and Beth sat them down and told them who the baby in the photo album was. That it was a baby girl Mark had fathered before he was married.

The fact that they all three of them knew that Mom existed was an extremely big deal for Mom. All of this time, being unable to find Diana, she began to feel like she didn't exist. But here were three people of her birth father's family that had always known she had existed, even before day one. Mom cried, finally quenching part of her desire to know her birth parents' real stories. It touched both of us that he had cared en-

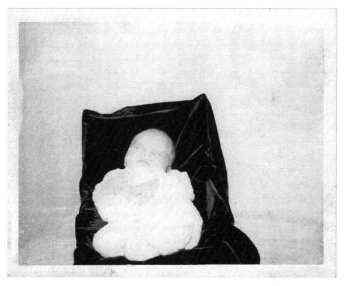

The photo of Cynthia shortly after birth that Diana sent to Mark. This photo was kept in Mark's family album with all the pictures of their other family members.

-ough to put her picture in the photo album with everyone else's. She wasn't just forgotten. He had probably done a double take at every little blonde girl he saw.

Beth told us how she and Mark always expected Mom to show up on their doorstep at some point. They felt that it was inevitable for her to come find them, obviously having no idea how much information the adoption agency kept from us. When Mark died in 2007, Beth figured Mom would never come. That there was no point in her coming now that her birth father was dead. Yet, if it hadn't been for his obituary, we would have never found him. I can tell you that for certain.

Sometimes, I think this is unfair, but I know that everything happens for a reason. Beth told us that she didn't know anything about Diana, or the other Duvalls, since they had moved away from Parsons rather quickly after Diana returned from the unwed mothers' home. This was in line with our paperwork, so we didn't question it. The adoption agency told us she was possibly in California, and it just reminded us of how far we still had to go to find her.

Beth told us a lot of stories about Mark and shared

scores of pictures. He sounded like a wonderful, outdoorsy guy, who loved to fish. He had a special nickname, which I will not share here because it may lead to someone recognizing his identity, and my goal is to give Beth and her children their well-deserved privacy, even as I share this story. I will say that his special nickname recognized his willingness to be responsible and help others whenever he could. Beth also affirmed that Mark had gone to the Catholic high school in town, which explained why he wasn't on my mom's notepad of possible boys from Parsons High.

Anybody reading this who knows my mother personally can vouch for her obsession with keeping things clean and organized to the nth degree. We decided she inherited that from Mark, after hearing Beth tell us of his hundreds of drawers that he built in the garage. Each of these drawers contained a very specific tool or other kind of material according to a very thorough organizational system. For example, he had separate drawers for AAA, AA, C, D, and 9 volt batteries.

Mom does have a battery section in one of her drawers, but she keeps them all together, which shows that Mark was even more organized than she is.

Nonetheless, it made Mom really happy to learn that she had inherited something from this man, that there was a similarity between their mannerisms. I think it proved to her that they really were related, and that she finally had someone to compare her life and personality with, something she had been lacking for many years. With all these stories and maybe a dozen pictures that we were sent over text message, Mom was dying to meet Beth in person. To make her feel more real, I think.

Now, my mother grew up in the Wichita area, and my grandparents lived around there for a long time to come. My grandpa owned a mechanic shop there. But, around 2001, they decided to move to Longview, Texas in order to take care of my great-grandparents for the last year of their life. This was a big change for our family, especially considering I was in the first grade at the time, but they needed to move for other reasons as well.

Many years passed before we saw my grandparents again, but in 2009, Mom, Matthew, and I decided that we would start traveling to Longview every year at New Year's. If you drew a line straight south from Kansas City, you would hit Longview. We decided that our annual trip might be the perfect time to take another trip to Parsons and find a meeting point with Beth. Christmas was nearly around the corner at this point.

By now, Mom was in contact with both Beth and Kris, Mark's younger sister closest in age to him that Mom had initially sent a letter to along with Steve, his brother. So, with excitement, we made plans to visit Parsons on the way down to Texas to meet Kris and meet Beth on the way home.

However, after Mom came down with pneumonia, we were unable to make our annual trip to Texas that year, and so we had to reschedule to the following spring break. Mom was crushed that she had to wait even longer.

Therefore, it wasn't until March of 2013 that Mom and I made our way to Parsons along our trip to Texas. Mom had not talked to Kris much, and so we were both very anxious as to what would happen and what we would learn. Mom was absolutely beside herself as we drove. I tried my best to keep her calm. It didn't work very well, but I couldn't blame her. This was the first time for her to go back to Parsons since 1992, two years before I was born.

We met Kris at the local Chinese restaurant. She was pale, thin, blonde, and in her mid-sixties. She was friendly, but not too friendly. As we ate our food, she had a handful of pictures to show us of Mark, Kris, the rest of their siblings, and of their parents. She had her own set of revelations for us, although not as big as Beth's.

It turned out that we had contacted the wrong people. Our biggest fear was that we would reveal a hidden secret and tear a family apart. That was why we decided to contact Mark's siblings over Beth, figuring that they were more likely to know; however, the truth couldn't have been more opposite.

Beth had known about Mom even before she was born, but Kris, Mark's sister closest in age to him, had never known. Not until Mom's letter popped up in her mailbox. Steve, Mark's brother who was also nearest to him in age, hadn't known either. None of the siblings had, but they feared that Beth was in the dark just as they were. However, Steve, Mark's brother, was extremely angry that Mark kept the secret of his baby from him and told Kris to ignore "any strange mail" she had received, thinking that we only wanted money. That was why neither of them responded to

Mom's letters. After some time passed, Kris ended up contacting Beth about it, and once learning that she knew, Kris reached out to my mom and offered to show us around Parsons.

Kris explained to us that her and Mark's parents would have likely murdered Mark if they had found out, and so that was likely why Mark never told his family. Mom and I felt terrible for altering Steve and Kris' relationships with their deceased brother, and it only made our worries run more rampant as we continued with our search.

After we finished our food, Kris gave us a tour of Parsons. She took us to the tiny, white house where all eight Workman siblings had grown up, as well as some other general landmarks in Parsons. At some point, we also visited the house where Diana had lived during her two years in Parsons, the address that was listed on Mom's original birth certificate. It was the house at the very end of the road, right next to the railroad tracks and directly underneath the city water tower. I couldn't imagine living in its shadow.

Kris also took us to the Catholic cemetery outside of Parsons, where Mark was buried. Kris left us at that point, in order to give Mom her personal time to mourn a father she never got to know.

The cemetery was out in the middle of nowhere. Only a handful of trees, surrounded by dry, Kansas grass. It was beautiful in its own sort of Midwest way. I tried to busy myself with the scenery to allow Mom her time. It was very hard for her to accept that he was gone, and that she would never get to meet him in person. She hopes to this day that she will get to meet him in heaven.

From Parsons, we continued on to Longview, Texas, where we stayed for three or four days, enjoying my mom's parents and extended family. They are truly wonderful people. It wasn't until our trip back to Kansas that we had arranged to meet with Beth, and her daughter, Nicole, at the Braum's in Mt. Pleasant, which was a nice halfway point from their home in Conway, Arkansas.

Mom was beyond nervous. Far more nervous than she had been when we were about to meet Kris. She wanted them to like her so badly. We pulled into the parking lot of that Braum's around eight or nine in the morning. They had just opened. Mom was armed with multiple photo albums when we walked through the front doors.

Sitting at the back of the restaurant among the midst of the smells of newly fried french-fries were two older women. A woman with her daughter, just as Mom and I were. There was no denying the resemblance between the two; Nicole definitely looked more like Beth than Mark. I don't remember how we greeted each other, but the talking began immediately. We actually didn't end up getting food for at least a couple of hours.

Beth and Nicole had brought all of their family albums, at least three or four good-sized ones. They had answers for every question my mom could think of, which have now escaped my memory. Beth was extremely open with us, as if she had known us our whole lives. I think Mom had to keep pinching herself to remind herself that this was real, and it wasn't a dream.

Mom used her phone to take pictures of everything she could. It reminded me of how she had begun her search with old yearbook pictures in 1992, taking a billion pictures of each one with her old film camera because she couldn't instantly see the pictures she had taken. Now, in 2013, she could take as many as she wanted without running out of space, or as few as she wanted because she could readily check the pictures she had taken. Smartphones are truly an amazing invention.

After another hour or so of endless talking, story-telling, and picture-exchanging, Mom and I knew that we needed to get on the road. We were still ten hours from home with my dad and little brother eagerly awaiting our return. Mom could have easily spent the whole day at that Braum's, but unfortunately, there was no way. We had brought two bouquets of flowers for Beth and Nicole, our thanks to them for meeting with us, so Mom ran out to the van to retrieve them. They were very surprised and thankful.

Mom and I can only hope that they know how much that visit meant to the both of us. To finally have real contact with people we had been trying to find for years was a wonderful, beautiful thing. As of the publication of this book, we have not seen Beth or Nicole again, but we are hopeful that we can see them again someday.

As we left that Braum's in Texas and drove home to Kansas City, we realized that a chapter of our search had come to an end. We had found Mom's birth father, Mark. We knew his story. We had met his widow and his daughter. We had seen nearly every picture ever taken of him and had constructed a true sense of what he was like as a person before he passed in 2007. In essence, our search for him was over. Mom's desire to know about her birth father and that half of her lineage was fulfilled, although to this day she continues to think of questions. Thankfully, she and Beth still text, and she can get those answers.

But now that we knew Mark's story, Mom's fierce desire to know Diana's burned brighter. We had found the birth parent that Mom thought would be the impossible of the two. Even though I had reached so many dead ends with Diana, Mom and I vowed that somehow, some way, we would find her. We would know her story, too.

I am so thankful we never gave up.

$\mathscr{C}$HAPTER 5:

FINDING MOTHER

$\mathscr{A}$ couple of months went by. It was May of 2013. As my semester at Emporia State wrapped up, I was very busy completing final projects and studying for exams. During the last two weeks of school, I decided to take a break from my schoolwork to try my searches for Diana again. By then, it had been a number of months since I had looked for her. However, a quick Ancestry search still rendered nothing. I even tried entering her birth date all by itself as I had done with Mark, but it gave me no results. Although, this at least affirmed to me that she was still alive. I never found an obituary for her.

A new thought struck me. She was alive; she wasn't dead. Ancestry kept leading me to dead ends because it was designed to search the past, not the present. I needed a way to search all of the living people in the United States currently, not decades ago. We had no idea what state Diana was in. She could be in Kansas still, in California where the adoption agency said she was, or even in Arkansas where her parents were buried. We had no real idea. Therefore, I discovered a new website called Peoplefinders.com, and entered Diana's first name, middle initial, and birth date. No last name. I needed every Diana in the U.S. that was born in 1949 if I was going to find her at this point.

There were thirteen results. Looking back now, I can't believe how few that is. God really helped us out there. Each one of the Dianas had a different last name and lived in a different place. I was overjoyed to finally have real names to search for. I wrote them all down, and then turned back to Ancestry or Facebook to cross-examine them.

From there, I narrowed them down similarly to how I had gone through Mom's list of high school boys who could possibly be her father. Pretty much all of them had the wrong birthday. Others had the wrong number or gender of siblings. Some of them had children whose birthdays conflicted with Mom's. I eventually got down to two or three of them that were all good options. I was afraid to get it down to one option. I was fearful it would be the wrong Diana.

In an attempt to narrow my search further, I decided to run the same kind of search for Donna, Diana's older sister. However, I didn't know her middle initial or exact birthday, only a possible two-year span. The search engine generated over one hundred results. Over one hundred women with the name Donna born in 1946 and 1947 still living in the United States. It was far too many to cross-examine.

At this point, I kind of ended up going down a rabbit trail. By now, the full 1940 Census had been uploaded to Ancestry, and I started researching Diana's father's previous wives more thoroughly. Mom's medical paperwork said that Diana and Donna had an older sister who lived in another state, so we had guessed that the family had moved to join her, most likely in California. I couldn't help thinking that if I could find this older sister, it would help me narrow down my two or three options for who Diana was.

While researching Clarence's second wife, Agnes Fahnert, I stumbled across the 1940 Census record of Agnes' mother, Mattie Fahnert. Agnes was absent, which fueled my belief that she had somehow died and her death record was missing (although I wouldn't find out until 2017 that she had passed in 2004. Whoops). More importantly, there was listed a "Carolyn Dewell", and my heart began to race. It had never popped up in my search before because the last name had been transcribed incorrectly. When I viewed the original document, the cursive handwriting clearly stated "Carolyn Duvall".

I couldn't believe it! However, this seemed to only dredge up more questions than answers. Her birthdate was listed as 1937, rather than 1941 like the medical paperwork said. That was too big of a difference to be a simple transcription error. Where was Carolyn's mother, Agnes? Why was Carolyn not with Clarence, her father? He had not left for World War II yet; I knew from my records. What had happened? I could not find a death record for Agnes for my life. After hours of searching every avenue I knew of, I had to put Carolyn and Agnes away. I had to remind myself that Diana was my focus, and the discrepancy in the birth date made me skeptical of Carolyn's being the other older sister Diana listed in her paperwork.

So, I returned to my list of potential Dianas, feeling downcast. However, everything changed when I noticed that one Diana on the list was living in Batesville, Arkansas. I immediately went back to my grave search website to double-check the record. Batesville was where Diana's parents, Clarence and Irene, were buried. What were the odds that a Diana J. born in 1949 was living in the exact town in Arkansas where her parents were buried?

I began to research the Diana in Batesville, Diana Robertson, on every platform I knew. I had accumulated quite a list of sites and resources to search with by this point, seeing as I had been searching on my own for about a year and a half. On most people search websites, the entry for a person will give you a handful of three or four other people commonly associated with the person you are searching for, and so I researched these people as well. Judging by their birth dates, I quickly deciphered which one was her husband and which ones were her children. The children were twins, and their birth date didn't conflict with Mom's.

I did every search I could think of before calling my mom. I double-checked every little fact I could. I tried to find this Diana on Facebook, but she didn't use it. I found her twin children who were now adults, and Facebook-stalked them to a whole new degree to try and find just one photo of their mother. Brian had pretty high security settings, so I could see nothing on his account. But Bridgett, on the other hand, had her settings a little more open to the public. All I wanted was to see a photo of their mother. I felt like that would be my proof just as it had been when finding Mom's birth father. But there wasn't a single picture of her. I even tried to find Donna on their Facebook accounts, but she was absent as well.

Once I exhausted my resources, I knew it was time to call Mom. Even if I couldn't tell her I was one hundred percent sure that this Diana Robertson was once Diana Duvall, I knew I needed to tell her that I had found my prime suspect. I remember closing the door to my dorm room, taking a deep breath, and plopping onto my bed with my phone. I remember not even greeting my mother when she answered, and just saying, "I may have found your mother."

Of course, Mom became super excited as I tried to relate to her everything I had found over the phone. We convinced each other more and more that we had found the right woman, but we were both still hesitant. We needed some sort of proof. But how could we get it? Arkansas was too far away for a day trip.

On one of the last few days of school, a week or so after I told Mom about Diana Robertson, I was sitting with my friends in another dorm room, enjoying their company before we all went our separate ways for the summer. That was when my phone rang. I noticed it was my mom and jumped up to dart back to my room to answer it, but nothing could have prepared me for what Mom had to say.

She had called Bridgett, Diana Robertson's daughter. She had posed as "her mom's old friend from high school" and asked Bridgett for her mother's maiden name. Bridgett responded, "Duvall."

It was her. Without a doubt, we knew that we had finally found a woman that we had tracked for almost exactly thirty years. Mom was overwhelmed with the information. She had searched for so long even before I came onto the scene that it was very hard to believe that we had at long last found this woman whose existence we sometimes questioned.

While it made me upset that my mother had lied to Bridgett about her real identity, I realized that we had suddenly come to the same crossroads we had faced with Mom's biological father's family. Did Diana's family know? If we contacted them, would we ruin a family forever? Split up a marriage? Destroy a relationship? Or, had they known all along and expected us to show up any time like Mark and Beth had? Last time, we had contacted Mark's siblings, Steve and Kris who were closest in age to him, but we couldn't find either of Diana's sisters, Donna or the elder one that I wasn't sure was Carolyn or not.

Meanwhile, time went by. I moved home for the summer and went back to work at the local Hy-Vee. Mom waited and prayed, trying to figure out what our best course of action would be. It felt a little bit like we were back at square one. We had found the woman, but had no idea how to contact her without isolating ourselves from her forever.

According to our records, Mom sent her first letter to Diana in June, which was written to be rather generic and vague. She left her first message on Diana and Duane Robertson's answering machine in September. This was all in 2013. We never received responses, which made the situation feel even more precarious.

Over the course of the next year or so, Mom wrote two more letters which were more specific. She told Diana who she was. What her life was like. Why she wanted contact so badly. At the very least, she wanted a more thorough medical history. My mother is a nurse, and I can't imagine being so well-versed in medical knowledge and yet having no idea what lies within your own genetic medical history.

Mom made it clear in all of her letters that she wasn't seeking money because of the last run-in with Steve, Mark's brother. She also sent Diana a picture of my family at my high school graduation in 2012, the most recent picture we had of my parents, my brothers, and myself. All of these letters, including two more phone calls, went unanswered. Again, we started to wonder if this woman actually existed.

It was easy to get busy in our lives and become lost in our waiting. I completed another year of college while Mom continued to be the awesome stay-at-home mother that she is to my dad and my younger brother. Life went on. Sometimes, I entirely forgot about our search. But Mom never forgot. Her desire to know wasn't quenched yet. It wouldn't leave her alone.

In the spring of 2014, we were met with a pleasant surprise from Nicole, Mark's daughter and Mom's half-sister. Her husband is rather into family history research just like I am, and he sent us a couple yearbook pictures that we had never seen before of not only Diana, but her husband, Duane Robertson.

It was her senior picture from Batesville High School in Arkansas, which further proved that we had found the correct Diana. She looked much older in this photo, far more than just two years from the only other picture we had of her as a sophomore in high school, but her smile was more genuine. And, as always, it felt like I was looking at a black and white image of my mother with a 60s hairstyle. Duane had a long face with dark hair and dark eyes. We had never seen what he looked like before. This was a big pick-me-up in our long time of waiting.

In December of 2014, after much prayer, waiting, and patience, Mom took the plunge. She was ready to take the next step and continue our search. It was time to try something new. She reached out to Bridgett, Diana's daughter, once more on Facebook.

It didn't go well. Bridgett had no idea Mom existed. She didn't believe us and reacted poorly. In the end, I don't really blame her. If a random stranger came up to me telling me that she was my mother's child from a previous man, I would think they were crazy, too. Mom sent her birth certificate as proof with Diana Jean Duvall's name emblazoned upon it. Bridgett told us that she needed time to absorb this brand-new information, as well as to talk to her twin brother, Brian. We knew this was going to be hard and possibly a shocker, so we were prepared to give her time to think about everything. We hoped she would get back to us.

As time went by, we were left unsure of how Bridgett was doing. She remained friends on Facebook with my mom, but she never contacted us again. To this day, Bridgett and Mom are thankfully still friends on Facebook. However, with no knowledge of Diana's health and fearful of her dying before we could make contact as what happened with Mark, we continued to try. Mom sent two more letters and made another phone call. It began to truly appear like we were being ignored, not simply catching them at the wrong time.

Luckily, it was only about a month before new information landed on our doorstep.

CHAPTER 6:

REJUVENATION

om informed Bridgett of her existence in December of 2014. While it was easy for Mom and I to once again fall away from our search due to the excitement of the holidays, it wasn't long before I made a huge discovery.

In January of 2015, I realized that I had never actually Googled the exact words "Diana Robertson Batesville AR". You have no idea how much I wish I would have done this sooner.

One of the very first hits was an obituary for Erlene Jines in Texas. As I began to read it, I wondered why Google had brought it as a result for me, until I reached the bottom. Nearly every obituary acknowledges the people who passed on before the individual as well as the people still living. For Erlene, this included not only Diana Robertson, but also Donna Magar.

I nearly dropped my laptop. I read the obituary at least five times to make sure I was reading it correctly and absorbing it fully. I had been skeptical that Carolyn, Clarence's daughter from his second marriage that I found on a Texas census, was the elder sister that Diana referenced in her medical history paperwork because of the difference in birth date. Erlene's birth date matched the one on the medical history, and I immediately knew that this was the right one. Erlene was the eldest sister that Diana had included in her birth history, not Carolyn, and Diana's mention in the obituary as her sister was proof.

However, that wasn't all. After searching for Donna, the middle sister, for years, the obituary finally revealed her married name. Magar. This was a whole new avenue for Mom and I to try. We were so fearful about contacting Diana's children because we didn't want to ruin their relationship with their mother, but, as far as we knew at the time from our paperwork, Donna had gone to the unwed mothers' home with Diana to keep her company. She already knew, so there was no possible way to ruin something between them. Contacting Donna quickly became our number one priority.

I searched for her vehemently. For an address, a phone number, a picture on Facebook, anything. I found Donna Magar within my earlier search of all the Donnas born in 1946 and 1947 still living in the United States, and thankfully there was only one with the unique last name. I studied the "Relatives/Associates" list of people on her profile diligently before searching her address and phone number on the Whitepages website to ensure that I found the right one. I wrote down the address and phone number excitedly. The search felt like it was so easy, and we were only a few phone calls away from finally making contact.

Unfortunately, things are never that simple. Mom tried calling Donna, but the phone number had been disconnected. Whitepages, while free and very useful, doesn't update their records very often. We did have an address so Mom decided to write a letter, but as time went by and Mom strove to make it perfect, it never made it to the mail.

The rest of 2015 went by quickly. By the time I found Erlene's obituary, I had become engaged. My family was thrust into the insanity of wedding planning, along with the milestone events of my graduation from Emporia State and my younger brother's graduation from high school. 2015 was a very busy year for the Riley family but one full of momentous, happy occasions. However, our search was becoming very cold.

In my free time, I tried researching the other people listed in Erlene's obituary, especially her son, Jeff Powell. I was ecstatic when I found him on Facebook in January of 2016 because he had a proclivity for posting old pictures with low privacy settings.

I Facebook-stalked him to the greatest degree I ever have in my entire life (if you're reading this, sorry Jeff!). I scrolled through years upon years upon years of status updates, profile picture changes, and other photos that I was able to see as someone who wasn't friends with him. I think I scrolled through the history of his entire account, but to my dismay, there were no pictures of Diana. There were a couple of

Brian and Bridgett, her children, whom we had already seen pictures of from earlier Facebook-stalking, but no Diana, or Duane, her husband, for that matter.

I found pictures of Jeff's mom, Erlene. She was very pretty, and I could see my mom in her from the beginning. Amazingly, I did find several pictures of Donna. There was a fifty-year difference between the pictures we previously had of her and the ones I found on Facebook, but there was no denying it was her. She was still beautiful, and while her hair was now white, she still had those dark eyes that reminded me of my mom.

I was living a little over an hour from my mom at this point now that I was married, so I started saving pictures to my computer from Jeff's Facebook account left and right. I saved multiple pictures of Jeff, Erlene, Donna, and the people that I was attempting to put together as Donna's children (Lisa, Tracy, and Scott). Then, I sent them all to my mom, some over text and some over e-mail, and that was a big moment for her.

Seeing Donna was the first time she actually got to set eyes on a Duvall in the present. Not a fifty-year-old high school photo of a person who seemed to have disappeared off the face of the planet. It made us feel like it may actually be physically possible to find Diana, or at least see a present-day picture of her as well.

We never tried contacting Jeff or any of Donna's children. As before, we were terrified that they didn't know and that it would ruin a relationship, as what happened with Bridgett. 2016 was filled with the loss of my grandfather and a lot of medical drama in my immediate family. We kept our focus on Donna, but the year was a busy one. Mom continued to take her time with her letter to Donna, wanting to word it perfectly and prayerfully thinking about it often. Thus, the letter was still placed on the backburner.

In the summer of 2016, I began graduate school, and my search halted completely. There was nothing more that I could do at this point, other than to be emotional support for my mom. I had researched everything I could research. I had found all three sisters listed in our documentation, and we had tried contacting the two who were still living. I had Facebook-stalked the grown children thoroughly, and saved so many pictures that they were hard to keep track of. Nevertheless, we still didn't have a picture of Diana, and we still didn't have contact. Mom's desire to know would not be satiated until that happened, and it began to occupy her every waking moment.

CHAPTER 7:

A MIRACLE

By January of 2017, Mom's desperation to know her birth mother was more than she could bear. She couldn't wait for a response from Bridgett or Donna any longer, so she did the only thing within her power to do. She very carefully crafted a message to Brian, Diana's son and Bridgett's twin brother, on Facebook. She tried so hard to get everything into one message, but once more, her message went unanswered.

Mom went through a rough period after this. She wore her heart on her sleeve and struggled with the notion that it may not be God's will for her to meet her birth mother. She began to beg Him to either intervene or heal her breaking heart. She was at a loss because we had finally reached the end of the line. There was nothing more to be done. She tried to talk herself into being okay with that, but it wasn't working.

Mom had also been sick for around three weeks, and she was terrified that Diana, her birth mother, would die before she could meet her. She didn't know if she could live with that, so she continued to beg God to help her. I supported her with everything that I could and was simply a shoulder to cry on via cell phone with more than an hour between us. In the end, it was between her and God.

To our awe, relief, and gratitude, God answered. On March 3rd, 2017, the absolute unthinkable happened. God worked a miracle for us.

On that day, Mom's old adoption agency contacted her, asking her to call them because they had some new information. Although, to be honest, it's a miracle that Mom even found their message. She was scrolling through Facebook on her phone as she always does before bed in order to wind down from the day, and her old Sunday school teacher's daughter had posted an update about checking your message requests on Facebook in order to protect your children against pedophiles. Mom decided to check hers, having never done so before, and was in for a shocker when she found a message from a woman who worked for her old adoption agency. If Mom had not seen that random post, the message from the adoption agency may have never been found.

Mom did not discover this message until Saturday, the 4th, and was forced to spend the whole weekend waiting for the adoption agency to open up again Monday morning. She was very antsy, but she was also trying not to get her hopes up. She called at exactly 8am, and we were blown away by what had occurred on their end just a week before.

The adoption agency had started going through their storage in order to digitize all their records. Now, all this time we had been told and fully believed that Donna had simply gone to the unwed mothers' home with Diana in order to keep her company. Nothing more. We were in for quite the shocker.

When the adoption agency started to digitize their records from 1965, they realized that they had two files that were extremely similar to each other. A

Donna Duvall and a Diana Duvall, of the same family and address, both had come to the unwed mothers' home and given up a baby girl in 1965.

Due to the similarities of the files, even down to their names, the adoption agency decided to contact Donna's daughter, Lisa, who was the contact person in her file. They wanted to ensure that the two files were digitized correctly, and they knew that Lisa had helped Donna find the baby she surrendered in 2010. They wanted to know if Lisa would like the information for Diana's child, someone that Lisa never knew existed.

When Mom called the agency bright and early Monday morning, she was told that Lisa was in a tizzy to talk to her. Before the end of the day, Mom and Lisa were in constant text messaging, and they spent hours on the phone throughout the week. I think I received hundreds of screenshots from those messages, and it was extremely difficult to keep up with all the new information we received. Our search had gone from stone cold to the fastest roller coaster ride in the span of twenty-four hours. God is so good!

It turned out that Donna had gone to the unwed mothers' home several months before Diana, in

January of 1965. In July, Donna gave birth to her baby girl and was sent home, while Diana was sent to the home in May and did not have my mom until December. Donna never even knew Diana was at the unwed mothers' home, because the girls were kept sequestered with other girls in the same month of pregnancy. This was far different than our belief that Donna had simply gone to the home to accompany Diana.

Donna and Diana's parents were very harsh and strict, as well as desperate to keep anyone from knowing they had two unwed, pregnant daughters, so both girls kept their secrets to themselves. All of their friends and family were told that Donna and Diana went away to take care of a sick aunt rather than to the unwed mothers' home. For years, Donna actually thought that Diana had a boy. It was a huge burden on them both.

In 2009, Lisa, one of Donna's daughters from her subsequent marriage, could tell that her mother was harboring a massive secret. Lisa urged Donna to tell her what was bothering her to help her get rid of her burden. As soon as Lisa found out that Donna had given up a baby girl in July of 1965, nothing could stop her from finding her. Donna called Diana to let her know that they were searching for Donna's baby and asked her if she wanted them to search for Diana's baby as well. She said no.

They found their baby, now a fully-grown woman called Jamie who lives in Wyoming, in 2010. It was slow-going at first, but Jamie and Donna have a speaking relationship now. The process was extremely cathartic for Donna, after holding such a heavy secret for so many years. It made her feel so much better that she called Diana to tell her the wonderful news and offered to help her find her baby again. Once more, to our dismay, Diana said "No".

But, because of how well this process had gone for Donna and Jamie, Lisa was ecstatic to talk to my mom and spread the catharsis. Soon, we both found ourselves in group text messages with Donna, Lisa, Tracy (Donna's other daughter), and Jeff, Erlene's son that I had Facebook-stalked so relentlessly. It was mindboggling to be in real conversations with these people that I had researched for so long and stared at their pictures wondering if we would ever meet.

Immediately, plans started circling about how we could all meet in person. Donna and Tracy were in

Arkansas, Lisa was in Tennessee, Jeff was in Colorado, and Mom and I were in Kansas. It was going to take some real planning, but Mom didn't waste any time beginning to ask the questions that had gnawed at her for longer than I've been alive.

We received pictures of Diana that we poured over for hours. Her resemblance to my mother was astounding. We saw her transform from her quiet high school senior photo into a young mom with twin toddlers and into an older woman at Erlene's funeral, which was held in 2006. This was the most recent photo they had of her.

We learned rather quickly that Diana wasn't a family person. She was an introvert and didn't ever call or come to family events, which is why their most recent photo was eleven years old. Mom was amazed that Diana became a nurse, since Mom had spent her career as a nurse, too. We were given a photo of Diana in her nurse's cap at graduation, and it was mind-blowing to compare it to Mom's graduation photo in her nurse's cap. What were the odds?

Diana still wants no contact at this point in time, even as I am typing these words. Brian and Bridgett, her children, have chosen to honor their mother's decision, and I don't blame them for that. Diana has only been recently made aware that Donna and her family have found us and met with us. However, at this point in time, Donna's family firmly believe that Diana's husband is unaware of my mom's existence, so it is rather likely that Diana will never want contact. We pray differently every day, but ultimately, we pray for God's will to be done.

Even though Diana's relationship was lacking with Donna's family, Donna and her family were very excited to meet us and didn't care if it hurt their pretty much nonexistent relationship with Diana or not. All of us compared our schedules for the summer and found the one weekend that all of us were available to travel. Plans fell together rapidly that we would all journey back to where it all began in order to meet for the first time: Hot Springs, Arkansas.

Mom counted down to our trip each day, and it wasn't long until we packed up to head southeast in June of 2017. As we hurtled along on the highway, it was incredible to remember where we were and where we were going. We were going to Arkansas. Not only were we going to meet Diana's family for the very first time, but we were going to see everything in Arkansas that we could possibly see from not only Diana's history but Mark's as well, Mom's birth father. It was a once in a lifetime trip, and one that we never dreamed we'd ever get to go on just six months prior.

$\mathcal{C}$HAPTER 8:

THE LAST LEG

$\mathcal{D}$ue to the fact that both of Mom's biological parents ended up in Arkansas after leaving the tiny town of Parsons, Kansas, she planned our trip to ensure that we could see everything we possibly could. She planned every minute of each day before we were slated to arrive in Hot Springs and meet everyone else.

Mom was so excited when she came to pick me up in Emporia. This was it. Our trip was finally here, and Mom was practically bouncing in her seat. After so many years of staring at maps of Arkansas towns and cities on her phone, we were about to go there in real life.

It took four or five hours to reach our first destination, which was the Bella Vista/Rogers area in northwestern Arkansas. Mom grew up with cousins and grandparents in Arkansas, so this was not her first time to the state, which she found to be rather ironic. We started off our trip of nostalgia by checking in on her grandparents' old house in Bella Vista, who had long since passed. The little old green house was nestled into a woody, hilly neighborhood, but we didn't stay long. Mom marveled at the changes it had undergone in the last twenty or thirty years, and then we moved on.

After staying the night at my dad's cousins' place in Rogers, we had a whole day in front of us to fill before having to be in Hot Springs that night. We zigzagged across the whole state, and for the hours in between destinations, Mom and I talked as I interviewed her for this book to make sure I had her part of her search straight. It had been such a long time since I'd asked her any questions that she told me some things I had forgotten a long time ago or had never known in the first place. It was a great bonding experience with my mom, even if we were stuck in a minivan for nearly twelve hours of driving back and forth.

Our first stop was the lake cabin that Mom's biological father, Mark, built with his own two hands. It was located in Shirley, Arkansas, and it was quite the adventure just to get to. We turned on the road which immediately turned into gravel. As we got further from the highway, it eventually dissolved into dirt and the steepest, downhill hairpin curves that I'd ever seen. It reminded me of when my husband I drove up and down Pike's Peak on our Colorado vacation in 2016.

Mom became concerned that we were lost, especially since her fancy navigation system said we had passed the lake house, but I was confident that we were going the right way. Sure enough, after a couple more daring curves, we passed a mailbox with the right number on it.

The little house was in the middle of nowhere, surrounded by trees. The lake was nowhere in sight, but Beth, Mark's widow, always called it the lake house. It was small and red, and whoever owned it now was adding on to it because there was a bit of construction.

We would have stayed longer, but a large dog began barking at us. Neither of us are really dog people, so, unnerved, we jumped back in the van and drove back up the intense, tight curves. Mom started becoming emotional for the first time during the trip, knowing that she was somewhere her birth father had been.

"I'm driving where he drove," she said, her voice quiet.

Our next destination was to drive by Diana's house, just to see if we could see anything. Now, here's the crazy part. There was only about twenty-five miles of highway between Mark's lake house and Diana's house. Mom's biological parents, at one time or another, were within only twenty-five miles of each other. We couldn't believe the odds of them meeting and conceiving a child in Parsons, Kansas, and then both of them, through the various courses of their adult lives, ended up in the same neck of the woods of Arkansas. Neither of us could get past the coincidence.

Alright, so I'll admit it. To be honest, Mom and I were planning on staking out down the road from Diana's house just to see if we could see her. See her come home with groceries or come get her mail. Nothing huge, we didn't plan on talking to her or anything. But, we drove right by her house without even realizing it.

Diana's home was on the outskirts of Batesville, and we had to turn around to go back. It turned out that the road listed as her mailing address is actually her very long, gravel driveway. We pulled in by her mailbox, but a big, livestock gate barred us from going any farther. Mom got out of the car to stand at the gate, looking to see if she could see the house from there, but she couldn't. The driveway was curvy and overgrown with trees and lush green leaves. Both of us inherently knew that we could not go past the gate. This was all the view we were going to get.

I didn't get out of the van. I let Mom have her space, because I knew she would need it. She stood at the gate for several minutes and rested her hand upon it. Then she walked back past the van and touched the mailbox for a few moments.

When she finally got back in the van, I looked at her quietly. She turned to me with glassy eyes and said in a warbling voice, "I touched where she touched." Then, she told me she needed a break from my interview, and we drove on.

Diana's house was only a few miles from Batesville, our next destination. First, we visited the local cemetery and found Diana and Donna's parents, Clarence and Irene Duvall. We paid our respects quietly, and soaked in the moment. We had truly found everyone even though it had felt like they didn't exist so many times along our journey. It felt crazy just to see the name "Duvall" carved in stone. After all, it had been such a process to find them.

After leaving the cemetery, we roamed the town to get a feel for it. It was small, but cute. We drifted around the downtown area, even though the main drag was under construction, looking for the movie theater that Diana's father, Clarence, had managed. It was his job that actually moved them around so many times. He started at the theater in Hot Springs, Arkansas, and was transferred to Parsons, Kansas in 1963. Then, in 1966, he was sent to Batesville, Arkansas, where they stayed.

We found the high school in Batesville as well, where Diana finished her schooling, before we realized the lateness of the day. Mom took a picture of her GPS to prove to herself later that she had truly been in Batesville, Arkansas, where her biological mother lived.

It was two or three hours southwest to Hot Springs where we were meeting Donna, Donna's daughters, Lisa and Tracy, her significant other, Larry, and Jeff, Erlene's son and Donna's nephew, for the first time. It was raining, but Mom and I kept our spirits up. After a small hotel dilemma, we found ourselves getting ready to meet these people that Mom had dreamt of meeting for so long.

Mom was having one of the worst panic attacks I've ever seen in my entire life. Breathing erratically, turning the A/C down in our room super low, and telling me to talk her down, she readied herself to meet her biological mother's family for the first time. These were people that she had been texting for about three months at this point, that we both had been stalking for over two years, and yet we barely knew them and they us. This was it, and first impressions carry quite a bit of weight.

Mom doesn't like elevators, so we walked down the stairs together. There was a group of people sitting in the lobby, waiting. While I'm not sure about Mom, my anxiety immediately melted away. They all greeted us with smiling faces and warm hugs, asking about our trip with their sweet, southern twang. After hours of talking and a supper of the largest pizza I've ever seen, it was easy for me to feel like we had been family all along.

The next two days were chock-full of adventures with our newfound family. We toured some gardens, a beautiful chapel, the downtown district, and drove through nature. More importantly, we received a family history lesson everywhere we went. We saw the hospital where Donna and Diana were both born, the house they grew up in, and both their elementary school and high school. We saw the theater their father, Clarence, managed during their time in Hot Springs, as well as the final resting place of their older sister, Erlene, Jeff's mother.

Later in the evening, they taught us how to play their family card game, Hand and Foot. It took a while for Mom and I to catch on, but thankfully we had great teachers.

During that time, we learned that Jeff knew all along that both his aunts had given up baby girls in 1965, something that not even Donna knew. After all my stalking of him over the years, I ardently wished that I'd had the guts to reach out to him. Perhaps, we could have made contact sooner. He had known for years, and I wonder, if the adoption agency had never decided to digitize their records, how long it would have taken for us to make contact with Jeff or Donna. But God's timing is perfect, so I try not to dwell on these thoughts.

It was far too soon before the extended weekend was over, and we found ourselves re-loading the minivan before we were ready. It was hard to say goodbye, but a lot of us had long roads ahead. It was an amazing experience and a fitting culmination of our decades-long search.

God truly blessed us with that trip to Arkansas. We were able to see everything we wanted to see and more, and we were lucky enough to have Mom's biological family show us around to get the inside scoop on everything. I know for certain that we will be seeing a lot of Lisa, Tracy, Jeff, Donna, and Larry in the future, because that bond will never be broken.

Shortly after we returned home from Arkansas, I came across an interesting bit of trivia. It turns out that Kansas is only one of five states in the United States of America that allow adult adoptees of my mom's generation to access their original birth certificate.

This shook me quite a bit because Mom's very first step in her search was acquiring her birth mother's name off of her original birth certificate. If we hadn't had that, I don't think our search would have ever gotten off the ground. It is just one more miracle that God worked for us so many decades ago to allow us to get started, because if Mom had been born in any of Kansas' neighbors, including Arkansas, she may have been unable to take the first step. We are so thankful for our search, no matter how hard it has been, because we were at least able to go on the journey in the first place.

EPILOGUE

So, there you have it. Every moment of our search for Mom's biological parents, Robert Mark Workman and Diana Jean Duvall. It was a long journey and a rough one. It was an experience that tested the limits of our endurance, our patience, and our faith.

I have no idea how many hours of computer time I have under my belt for this project, but I am confident that it numbers in the hundreds, if not the thousands. This search is thirty-four years old, which is more than a decade older than I am. While the search did not end the way we once hoped, we wouldn't trade the blessings that came of it for anything.

What now? For now, our search is complete. There is nothing more that we can do. We have met so many wonderful people that have adopted us back into their families, even if we can never speak to Mark, may he rest in peace, or Diana. Our desire to know has mostly been fulfilled. We learned their stories. We learned their lives. We learned the reasons behind the decisions they made, and Mom no longer wonders what it would have been like if she had never been put up for adoption.

In the end, Mom is simply overjoyed to have such great contact with both sides of her biological family. She can text or call them whenever she wants and can ask her questions freely. Questions she once felt like she had to hide or would never know the answers to. She finally has a mostly up-to-date family health history for the first time in her life. We are really very happy with how well everything has turned out, and we give God all the glory of bringing our search to an end.

Now, when I say our search is at an end, I mean it in the very specific sense of those words. We no longer have to search. We have contact with both sides of the family, relationships with both Mark's widow and daughter, as well as Diana's sister and her family. We know where Mark is and where Diana is. We know what happened to them both after they surrendered their baby girl for adoption in 1965.

However, I don't think that I can say that the journey itself is over, because I know my mother's desire to know will never be one hundred percent satisfied. She will always think about Mark and wonder what it would have been like to meet him. Currently, she is hoping to hear a recording of his voice if Beth can find one.

Likewise, she will always stare at the map of Batesville on her phone. She will always pray that perhaps someday Diana will change her mind about not wanting contact. Is this in vain? I don't know, but it never hurts to pray. Little things like this will probably continue to follow Mom for the rest of her life.

Nonetheless, this process has taken on a new meaning for my mother. For years, people around her have asked, "Why are you doing this?" or "What do you expect to get out of this?". In the beginning, before I took over the search, Mom used to respond that it just made her happy. It made her happy to search for her birth parents and discover their stories. To know them, in the best way possible.

It is far more than that now. Instead of just making her happy, Mom has emotional connections to her birth parents today. She has journeyed from Kansas to Arkansas, just as they both did. She has driven the road that her father drove and touched the gate that her mother touched. Her birth parents are no longer phantoms of her past, people that we often wondered if they even existed and were nothing more than whited-out names on a sheet of paper. Thanks to our search, they are real people. People we know and harbor in our hearts, even if one has passed on from this world and the other has not opened her heart to us.

Through it all, the most amazing part has been the fact that my mother and I were able to walk this journey together. That I was able to help her complete this finding of her identity while most of the people in her life simply shook their head or never understood its importance to her. It has resulted in a relationship between us that is far more than just mother and daughter, and for that, I will forever be grateful. Our bond will always last regardless of whether this is the last page of our story or not. After all, only God knows.

The End

(for now)

$\mathscr{T}$IMELINE

September 1946 – Robert Mark Workman is born in
    Parsons, KS.

August 1949 – Diana Jean Duvall is born in Hot
    Springs, AR.

1963 – Clarence Duvall, Diana's father, is moved
    from the Hot Springs movie theater to the
    Parsons one. Mark and Diana begin to date.

January 1965 – Donna, Diana's elder sister, is sent to
    the unwed mothers' home in Wichita, KS.

May 1965 – Diana is sent to the same unwed mothers'
    home.

July 1965 – Donna gives birth to her baby girl, later

named Jamie, and is sent home to Parsons.

December 1965 – Diana gives birth to her baby girl, who later becomes Cynthia May Giger, and is sent home to Parsons.

January 13, 1966 – Diana's baby girl is adopted to Raymond and Gracie Giger in Wichita, KS.

Early 1966 – Shortly after both girls return home, the Duvall family moves once again to a different movie theater in Batesville, AR.

December 1966 – Mark marries Beth in Parsons, KS.

1983 – Cynthia turns eighteen years old and requests her original birth certificate.

1986 – When transferring to a new nursing school, Cynthia pays her adoption agency for her health history form.

1990 – Cynthia updates her information with her agency after her marriage.

1992 – Cynthia travels to Parsons to find a picture of her birth mother in a high school yearbook and come up with a list of possible birth fathers.

1994 – Michaela, Cynthia's daughter and author of this book, is born.

1999 – One of Cynthia's nursing students reveals to

her that there is a Catholic high school in Parsons, which was where her birth father likely attended.

2007 – Mark passes away of leukemia.

2009 – Donna reveals to her daughter, Lisa, that she gave up a baby girl in 1965. They decide to search for her and call Diana to ask if she would like them to search for her baby (Cynthia), too. Diana says no.

2010 – Donna and Lisa find Jamie, her surrendered baby, and begin a cathartic relationship with her. Diana is asked again if she wants to look for Cynthia, but she says no once more.

July 2011 – Michaela becomes interested in family history and purchases her first Ancestry membership. Once completing her ancestral research, she begins on her mother's birth parents.

October 2011 – Michaela finds grave records for Clarence and Irene Duvall, Diana's parents.

November 2011 – After reaching a dead end on Diana, Michaela switches her focus to discovering Cynthia's birth father by using the list of names Cynthia found at PHS.

December 2011 – Michaela stumbles across Mark's obituary, and all the details fit.

Early 2012 – Cynthia writes letters to Steven and Kris, Mark's siblings closest in age to him.

March 2012 – Cynthia asks to be friends with Beth, Mark's widow, on Facebook.

July 2012 – Michaela begins to search for Diana again. Cynthia creates a Facebook group to search for her.

September 2012 – Beth approves Cynthia's friend request. They begin to talk.

March 2013 – Cynthia and Michaela travel to Parsons to meet Kris, Mark's sister, during their annual trip to Texas, and meet with Beth and Nicole on their way home.

May 2013 – Michaela begins to search for Diana in a new way and discovers a potential match. Cynthia calls the potential person's daughter, Bridgett, and confirms that it is truly her.

June 2013 – Cynthia writes her first letter to Diana.

September 2013 – Cynthia leaves her first message on Diana's answering machine.

2013-2014 – Cynthia writes two more letters.

Early 2014 – New photos of Diana and her husband,

Duane, during high school are sent to Cynthia.

December 2014 – Cynthia contacts Bridgett on Facebook to tell her that she is Diana's daughter who was given up for adoption in 1965.

January 2015 – Michaela discovers a new obituary for Diana's eldest sister, Erlene, which reveals Donna's married name. Cynthia writes a letter.

January 2016 – Michaela finds Erlene's son, Jeff, on Facebook. He has several pictures of Donna, her family, Erlene, and Diana's children.

January 2017 – Cynthia begins to struggle with the fact she may never have contact with Diana, her birth mother. She tries to contact Brian, her son.

March 2017 – The adoption agency messages Cynthia to tell her that Lisa, Donna's daughter, wants contact with her.

June 2017 – Cynthia and Michaela travel to Arkansas to see special locations and to meet Donna's family and Jeff for the first time. Michaela interviews Cynthia for this book.

August 2017 – Donna tells Diana that she met Cynthia.

$\mathcal{F}$REQUENTLY $\mathcal{A}$SKED $\mathcal{Q}$UESTIONS

$\mathcal{D}$ue to the extensive nature of this search, we have decided to include a FAQ section for common questions we have been asked along the way. Also, we hope that this section can serve as a resource and encouragement for other adoptees searching for their birth parents.

Q: What resources did you use to find Cynthia's birth parents?

A: More than I could count. Each tended to serve a different purpose. My mother did a lot with what she had in the 80s and 90s, but the Internet was truly our big breakthrough. I used Ancestry, Whitepages, Legacy, Peoplefinders, Peoplelookup, Peoplesearch,

Facebook, Findagrave, Classmates, and possibly more. I used them to find historic documents detailing their parents, addresses, phone numbers, possible relatives, cemetery records, obituaries, yearbook photos, and more. Everything was like one small puzzle piece that either added to the picture we were trying to construct or couldn't fit in and had to be thrown out. I am sure the Internet will only continue to evolve as far as these resources go, so if you find yourself trying to find a birth parent, make sure not to limit yourself by using just one website.

Q: How helpful was Ancestry? Is the membership worth it?

A: Ancestry was extraordinarily helpful, but it has its limitations. It is wonderful if the person you are searching for is more than seventy-two years old. This is because United States law only allows a federal census to be released to the public once it is seventy-two years old. For example, the 1950 Census will not be released until 2022. Ancestry was great to get a lot of information about Mom's birth parents' parents (her birth grandparents), but not really her parents themselves.

Q: Adoption is a private thing. What if they don't want to be found? Don't you think they did what was best for their baby?

A: While conducting our search, this was on our

minds at all times. We have done our best to be respectful of their wishes. While Mom knows that adoption was what was best for her, there was no changing the fact that she was curious. She wanted to know her origins, and I believe she had the right to feel that desire to know. Therefore, we conducted our search with the utmost care, often waiting years in order to not be considered pushy. Even to this day, we are respecting Mom's birth mother and not pushing her into contact.

Q: How long has Cynthia known she was adopted? How did her parents tell her?

A: Mom has always known she was adopted. There was no time when it was considered a secret, not even when she was little. Therefore, her parents never had to tell her. It was always common knowledge.

Q: Is the search worth it?

A: Most definitely. Even if it doesn't turn out the way you once thought, it is still cathartic to not have to wonder anymore. You don't have to wonder what happened or where they are or why they gave you up anymore. There is a peace that comes with finally knowing all the answers.

If, by chance, we did not answer the question plaguing you, please feel free to contact us through our publisher!

ACKNOWLEDGMENTS

First off, I'd like to thank everyone who ever told me that this experience deserved to be a book! It is thanks to you all that this book has finally found its way into print.

As always, thanks to my husband, Olin, who continues to support me in all that I do and encourages me to write. Thank you also to my parents and my brothers, who are always there for me, even from miles away.

Even more so, I'd like to thank Mom and I's new family members. Your names may not be in here for everyone's privacy, but I cannot thank you all enough for accepting us into your family. Thank you for all your help and for being willing to answer any question at any time via text message. You all rock, and I can't wait until Mom and I can make another trip to visit you all.

To all that helped shape this book into its final form, thank you! Daphne Evans, Cynthia Riley, and Hannah Robinson, you are all fabulous editors and beta readers. I don't know what I would do without you! You make my writing shine.

Also, thank you again to Magpie Designs, Ltd. for the amazing cover! You continue to blow me away by creating something amazing out of my rambling emails.

Almost last, but not least, I must thank my mother's birth parents. My biological grandparents. I haven't had the privilege to meet either of you, but neither my mom or I would be here without you two. Rest in peace, Mark, and you will always be in my prayers, Diana.

Finally, thank you, Reader! A small town author such as myself appreciates your support so very much. I look forward to continuing my writing career with you!

ABOUT THE AUTHOR

Michaela Riley Karr was raised in Olathe, KS and received her master's degree in English from Emporia State University in 2017. She now lives in rural Emporia, KS with her husband, Olin, on a goat ranch. She is also the author of *The Story of the First Archimage* series.

Scan the QR code below to visit her website and learn about her other writings and events!

www.michaelarileykarr.wordpress.com

Proof

Made in the USA
Columbia, SC
21 November 2017